MULTI-LEADERSHIP IN URBAN SCHOOLS

Shifting Paradigms for Administration and Supervision in the New Millennium

Judy A. Alston

University Press of America,® Inc.
Lanham · New York · Oxford

Copyright © 2002 by
University Press of America,® Inc.
4720 Boston Way
Lanham, Maryland 20706
UPA Acquisitions Department (301) 459-3366

PO Box 317
Oxford
OX2 9RU, UK

ISBN 0-7618-2420-0 (paperback : alk. ppr.)

Dedication

This book is dedicated to my parents, George and Naomi Alston and to the memory of my late grandmothers, Wilhelmina Swinton and Janie Forrest who always remind in spirit and in flesh that I can do anything that I put my mind to and to just live.

Contents

Preface

In 2000 I attended the American Educational Research Association's annual meeting, held in New Orleans, LA. As per my usual conference participation, I went to a number of sessions, but one in particular inspired the genesis of this text. This roundtable paper discussion highlighted the necessary components for creating safe environments for schools and what the role of the principal would be in creating such settings. As the discussion ensued with the five or six participants, my musing began to give form to a concept that the principal, as one person, could not effectively run a school building in the 21st century.

Reminiscent of my experiences as a classroom teacher, often taking on administrative duties, I had witnessed that it was difficult for one person to *really* do all the jobs that he or she was required to do as principal. So as my colleagues continued to discuss the paper, I had an epiphany—one school level administrative post, the principal, could be apportioned into three separate people—three separate and distinct assignments and responsibilities—three separate and distinct titles.

I began to think back to previous conversations with colleagues and students in the education and supervision courses that I had taught, and remembered that the idea of the Chief Knowledge Officer had become a part of earlier discussions. At first I was enamoured with the meaningfulness the term evoked. I then began to make connections between the Chief Knowledge Officer and the building level principal. I contemplated--the Chief Knowledge Officer and the principal – how would this role develop in administrative leadership? One thing became very apparent as I read the literature, worked with many principals in urban and rural settings, and continued my teaching and research in educational administration and supervision--that one of the most important jobs of every principal is that of instructional leader. Unfortunately, in most cases the principal is not given the opportunity to really be an instructional leader in his or her school because of the time consuming day–to-day operations. The focus toward curriculum and instruction each school day is often deflected by the many other parts of the school culture. Some principals are aware of how difficult it is to focus in on the instructional component of the school day and quite frankly some are not comfortable with the pedagogical charge related to the principalship.

Almost immediately I sat there and I started to draft out in my mind and eventually on a piece of paper what a "three-headed" principal would look like. I thought it appropriate to have a Chief Knowledge Officer (CKO), someone to focus on the curricular and instructional leadership in a school. The second person would be a Chief Operational Officer (COO), a person in charge of the daily school functions, maintenance issues, bell schedules, bus breakdowns, and discipline issues. These are the things reported by many principals that take an inordinate amount of their workday. Using the terminology of business in education is often contested in some educational arenas; however, I found this aspect of a business model befitting to what I am endeavoring to do with this text.

Consideration of the fiscal challenges of schools in this 21st century–the disparity of wealth in school funding—the model needed to include a Chief Financial Officer (CFO). Recent observations reveal many areas in the country are experiencing difficulty in passing school bonds and operational levies. Given the move to increase decentralization and looking at local control at the school level with the principal in charge, schools need a CFO to deal with the school general budget fund and external funding opportunities.

Consolidation of each of these concepts gave birth to the Alston Multi-leadership Model, (Chief Knowledge Officer; Chief Operations Officer, and Chief Financial Officer, CFO) for urban schools in particular but with broader application for school administration in general. Thus we have the whole notion of the three headed principal, three distinct people doing three distinct jobs but all participating in a model of leadership that can contribute to the creation of a community of learning that will improve delivery of instruction and maximize student opportunities for academic excellence.

As the years have passed since 2000 I could not come up with the intricate details of the actual model or with a visual representation that best depicted both the simplicities and complexities of the design. In the autumn of 2001, as I was driving my daily twenty minute commute from the campus of Bowling Green State University, a vision, if you will, came to me and a feasible representation of the model appeared. Soon I put pen to paper, or as 21st century technology would have it, I struck the keys on the computer keyboard and fully developed the multi-leadership model.

I anticipate this book will offer direction, guidance and be a blessing to a "seasoned" or new colleague in the field of educational administration. May we together continue in this work, dedicated to academic success for all children as part of effective leadership teams remembering the words of King Solomon, once lauded as the wisest leader among his contemporaries:

Two are better than one because they have a good reward for their labor. For if they fall, one will lift up his companion, but woe to him who is alone when he falls, for he has no one to help him up... Though one may be overpowered by another, two can withstand him and a threefold cord is not quickly broken. (Ecclesiastes 4: 9-10, 12 [NKJV])

Acknowledgments

This book would not have been written without the prayers and help of many people and I would just like to say thank you to all that have been there for me during this process.

Thank you to my colleagues in the Program in Educational Administration and Supervision and the Doctoral Program in Leadership Studies at Bowling Green State University. Special thanks to Mrs. Karen Gerkens, "secretary extraordinaire." As well as to Dr. Patrick D. Pauken whose limitless knowledge and sense of humor both help make my job a little better every day. Also, thank you to the ladies in the Word Processing Center in the College of Education and Human Development at Bowling Green State University: Judy Maxey and Sherry Haskins for their help with the manuscript.

Thank you to my friends across the country who have been supportive and encouraging.

Special thanks to some people who hold very inimitable places in my heart:
- Charnita Y. Gladman – My best friend (who always understands me even when I don't).
- Sharyn N. Jones – Graduate Assistant; Soror; Friend like no other; I'm so very proud of who you are.
- Tanya L. Sharpe – Friend; Soror; Supporter; Words could never express...THANK YOU!
- Carl and Christopher Stewart – "my boys" (now young men) who just love the child in me.
- Rhea N. Young – A good friend who read and helped to edit the whole thing.

Very special thanks to my friend Dr. Cynthia A. Tyson who typed, read, and listened when I just couldn't and didn't want to anymore. This book would not have been written without your help, support, and encouragement –"When anxiety was great within me, your consolation taught joy to my soul" (Ps. 94:19 [NIV]). Thank you for pushing me to the limits and for living and loving the metaphors.

Most importantly, to the One who gave me and made me everything that I have and am—my *Heavenly Father*—who sustains me with the knowledge that I can do all things through Him.

Chapter 1

What Is Multi-leadership?

Wanted: A miracle worker who can do more with less, pacify rival groups, endure chronic second-guessing, tolerate low levels of support, process large volumes of paper, and work double shifts... to innovate, but can not spend much money, replace any personnel or upset any constituency. (Fullan, 1998)

Insurgency and support of effective leadership have historically determined the establishment of many countries. In many nations democracy is contingent on the varied characteristics of good leadership (illustrated above) as evidenced in the many appointments to leadership positions in the government, the military, corporations, and education. Schools, in particular, with various patterns of administrations, and the diverse roles of educational leadership are not immune. Much like the upstart of a *young democratic* nation, strong administrative leadership is essential to the stable operation of a school. Cries are heard about the lack and poor quality of leadership in our public schools, particularly the large urban schools districts. In describing leadership, one must look at the gaps between theory and practice, the difference between what one thinks and teaches, the issues about power and change, as well as about the connection of dreams to reality. In some respects, leadership can be likened to art appreciation—for some artistic expressions are hard to understand—and sometimes arduous to appreciate, but we still form opinions of what we feel is good and bad. While students, teachers, caregivers and community members all have opinions of what is good and bad leadership, leadership in some school settings requires a broad base of understandings, but it is that breadth of perspective that is often difficult to appreciate.

Traditional Notions of Leadership and The Principalship

> The need was never so great. A chronic crisis of governance—that is, the pervasive incapacity of organizations to cope with the expectations of their constituents—is now an overwhelming factor worldwide. If there was ever a moment in history when a comprehensive strategic view of leadership was needed, not just by a few leaders in high office but by large numbers of leaders in every job, from the factory floor to the executive suite, from McDonald's fast-food franchise to a law firm, this is certainly it. (Bennis and Nanus 1985, 2)

Leadership has been defined as "the process of influencing others to achieve mutually agreed upon purposes for the organization" (Peterson, 1987, 3). It involves influencing one or more people in a positive way so that the tasks determined by the goals and objectives of an organization are accomplished. The leadership role can either be assigned or assumed. It has a complex blend of behaviors, attitudes, and values, and can occur in a small organization where everyone is known or in a complex bureaucracy where few people in a department even know each other (Hart 1980). It has also been defined in terms of individual behavior, influence over other people, interaction patterns, role relationships, occupation of an administrative position, and perception of others regarding legitimacy of influence (Yukl 1991).

Historically, leadership has been viewed as a characteristic or distinguishing feature, quality, or attribute possessed by people that enable them to effectively accomplish goals (Cook 1930; Tead 1930). In recent years, it has been defined more as a process and can include the concepts of creating action, promoting empowerment and growth, or involving the interaction between leaders and followers. Leadership is a concept central to theories of how organizations such as schools and educational bureaucracies work (Blackmore 1989). As a process, the definition of leadership includes the concept of creating action. Also, through the process, followers are empowered to achieve and to grow individually as well as to work toward a common goal within a group (Christ 1994).

Various qualifications, attributes, characteristics, and skills have been studied and described by researchers on what makes an effective or successful leader (Alston 1999; Alston and Jones 2002; Chapman 1993; Dinham, Cairney, Craigie, and Wilson 1995; Owens 1995; Sergiovanni 1996; Smith and Holdaway 1995; Thurston, Clift, Schacht 1993; Vandenberghe 1995; and Zhang 1994). Owens (1995) has noted that leadership is a group function and that leaders purposely seek to influence the behavior of others. Our understandings of school leadership and school leaders are dependent upon the relationships between school leaders, school climate, school culture and the community the school serves.

Leadership is taking risks, making mistakes and learning from these mistakes. Leadership provides the very foundation for a sound educational program. When the leadership is right, people are inspired to do their best.

Patterson (1984) described leadership as "the process of influencing others to achieve mutually agreed upon purposes for the organization" (p. 57). In particular, when focusing on leadership practice in urban schools—schools located in central cities of metropolitan areas and serve children who are socially and academically at risk (Urban School Services 2002), we see a need for promethean change. Despite the often innovative efforts for urban reform, we have failed to successfully educate children living and attending schools in these areas (Lomotey 1989). Urban schools indeed face several problems and challenges that are the result of city dynamics. Urban schools must deal with inadequate educational resources, red tape and administrative bureaucracy, and a negative perception of city school children (Ayers 1994; Weiner 1999). Aquila and Parish noted, "As urban schools have become consistently less effective, community and parental support for them has declined...The less effective they become and the more they believe that they are helpless to do anything about it" (p. 229). This places considerable pressure on the traditional urban school principal. For example, in these metropolitan districts public housing in individual school attendance zones often create larger than code specified school building capacity. This overcrowding can increase the challenges that larger, impersonal interactions can present, and often uncover many roadblocks for the principal (Sarason 1982). In order to regain effectiveness, new paradigms and methodologies are needed to truly improve education (Ash and Persall 2000).

While there pragmatically can not be a uniform, one size fits all *recipe* for effective educational leadership, there can be a *blueprint*

4 Multi-leadership in Urban Schools

with different theoretical conceptualizations that promote practical application in support of goals to improve student achievement—"by any means necessary." Urban school leadership in this new century can not continue to follow the same paths of tradition that it has for the last 50 years. Riggins (2001) stated:

> Today's urban principalship has become increasingly more demanding as the spectrum of responsibilities—instructional leadership, relations with staff, parents, and community; recruitment, hiring, and retention of teachers; staff development and evaluation; and budget and facilities management—continues to widen. Added to these responsibilities are duties unique to the urban principalship, such as developing a multicultural focus to the curriculum, combined with strategies for inclusive instruction and behavioral interventions. Consider as well the need to maintain adequate support mechanisms for families in poor and highly diverse communities, and to involve parents of those families in their children's education. (p. 27)

These are some of the same issues that Fredericks (1992) noted regarding the five major challenges for today's urban principals

> ➤ Effectively dealing with reform and restructuring through a process of group development and consensus;
> ➤ Meeting the social and educational needs of students;
> ➤ Implementing meaningful systems of staff development and empowerment;
> ➤ Facilitating the identification and implementation of meaningful school goals; and
> ➤ Evaluating progress to make appropriate midcourse adjustments.

Sanders (1999) echoed these challenges as he noted that for the urban principal any aspect of school reform or restructuring is strongly influenced by the socioeconomic and institutional environment within which the school exists.

Multi-leadership: A Model

Various researchers have suggested differing types of styles of leadership and traits that effective leaders possess. However, in my experiences with K-12 educational leadership, (both teaching and research), few in fact address the needs of large urban school districts in this new millennium because they continue to subsist in a historical paradigm that is largely ineffective when met with contemporary challenges facing these schools.

An emerging concept that speaks to the needs of the multiple layers of responsibility related to school administrative effectiveness is *co-leadership.* Co-leaders in an organization are central individuals who work together with shared objectives and aspirations toward a common goal (Heenan and Bennis 1999). They accept the **responsibility for** and the **leadership of** the organization. Co-leaders share "affection, trust, and commitment to a common enterprise. Labor is divided easily, according to gifts of both parties. Disagreements are resolved without acrimony and without loss of mutual respect" (Heenan and Bennis 1999, 263).

Co-leadership in the principalship is not a new idea. Drake and Roe (1999) noted that the idea of a *co-principalship* could provide interactive support between two or more professionals as well as emphasizing the purpose of the school. Furthermore, Kennedy (2001) saw that "...it is time to divide the principalship into two positions—instructional leader and building manager" (p. 60). A response to the paradigmatic shifts in educational leadership as it relates to school-based decision making, total quality management, restructuring schools curriculum and instruction, issues with equity, diversity, safety, security, school funding and finance is the *Alston Model for Multi-leadership.* This exemplar for reform—multi-leadership—involves a three-pronged principalship: the Chief Operating Officer (COO), the Chief Financial Officer (CFO), and the Chief Knowledge Officer (CKO). These three individuals (see Figure 1.1) would work as equals fulfilling the role of the *principal* of the school.

Figure 1.1 Alston Model of Multi-leadership

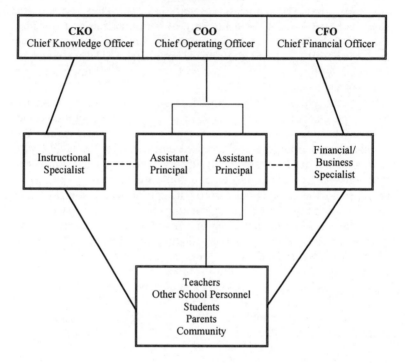

THE PRINCIPAL

CKO Chief Knowledge Officer	COO Chief Operating Officer	CFO Chief Financial Officer

Instructional Specialist --- Assistant Principal | Assistant Principal --- Financial/ Business Specialist

Teachers
Other School Personnel
Students
Parents
Community

The quality of urban, rural, suburban and private education depends on the quality of its leadership. Effective leadership is synonymous with schools that operationally run smoothly and are communities of learning that maximize student possibilities for excellence in academic achievement.

Shared leadership—a multi-leadership model best serves the needs of urban schools. The greater the expertise of individual people involved in leadership roles, the more sustainable the results of effective leadership can be. Schools need to be envisioned as a community of leaders—a place whose very mission is to ensure that students, parents, teachers and administrators all become leaders in some way (Barth 1988).

This idea of multi-leadership is not very far off of the beaten path of the current view of and practice in the principalship. For example, Sergiovanni, Burlingame, Coombs, and Thurston (1999) noted the following regarding the roles for which principals opted:

> Some stressed their role as instructional leaders. They saw the principalship as the key role for the improvement of classroom teaching. Others sought to be both instructional leaders and effective bureaucrats. These principals sought to fulfill both functions. Still others stressed the administrative and played down the instructional. For these bureaucratic principals, the classroom was the province of the teacher; the principal entered that classroom as few times as possible. Teaching was an individual art form that could not be improved by meddling by the principal. In turn, the hallways were the provinces of the principal. The principal built the school schedule, set the general standards for decorum and discipline and, in general, decided the policies of the school—so long as they did not directly conflict with the classroom. (p. 200)

Successful schools are led by strong principals (Kimbrough and Burkett 1990; Lomotey 1989; Edmonds 1979); indeed, they are organizations that depend on strong leadership. In most American K-12 schools, the building principal is undoubtedly the "leader" of the school. As the school's leader, the principal assumes numerous responsibilities, such as financier, disciplinarian, instructional leader, and facility manager. However, as the challenges of schools continue to change, models for shared power and governance structures become increasingly important. Change in the world is inevitable and leadership is no exception (White, Hodgson, and Cramer 1996). Furthermore, change in leadership is not only about how leadership is defined, but also about how people practice leadership (Drath 1998).

21st Century School Leadership

Beck and Murphy (1993) have noted various metaphors chronicling how this role of the principal has changed over the past 70 years. They indicate that the principal of the 1920s and 1930s was the spiritual leader, the scientific manager, and the social and dignified leader. In the 1940s this person was the leader on the home front, the democratic leader, the curriculum leader/supervisor, and the public relations representative. In the 1950s the principal became more of an administrator who defended educational practice, managed time efficiently, and was the overseer of minute details. In the 1960s the principal wore the hat of the bureaucrat, the user of scientific strategies, and the inhabitant of a role in conflict. The 1970s ushered in a concept of the principal as community leader, imparting meaning, a juggler of multiple roles, and as a facilitator of positive relationships. By the 1980s the principal became the problem solver/resource provider, an instructional leader, a visionary, and a change agent. Finally, in the 1990s and into the turn of this century, the principal is seen as leader, as servant, as organizational and social architect, as educator and moral agent, and as a person in the community.

The changes regarding school leadership in the past decade have provided a unique opportunity to reformulate our thinking about all aspects of public education. "School leadership's function is to mobilize people to change how they themselves work so that they collectively serve to better the emerging needs of children and demands of society" (Donaldson 2001, 8). Effective school improvement many times translates into better student outcomes. Firestone (1996), Schlechty (1997), and Short and Greer (2002) all agreed that the best way to begin conceptualizing restructured schools is with how students learn. Thus, this notion of school reorganization (in this case school administrative reorganization) and effective leadership with a view to how administrators can best lead will be significant.

For instance, with the advent of site-based management, more principals will have to spend a larger percentage of their time engaged in activities in which they are autonomous and are acting as superintendents of their own buildings (Daresh 2002). In many cases, the principal of a large urban secondary school has the jobs of supervising a large teaching and support staff, managing a large budget, dealing with public relations, participating in all major school events as well as service and other organizations, and ensuring that all federal, state, and local requirements are met (Armstrong, Henson, and Savage 2001). These demands are unbelievable and the accountability in education today is unprecedented. "In a world of increasing interdependence and ceaseless technological changes, even the greatest of Great Men or Women simply can't get the job done alone. As a result we need to rethink our most basic concept of leadership" (Heenan and Bennis 1999, 5). **An understanding of what we as individuals epistemologically define as *school* must be in solidarity in this new century, with the idea of *school* as a multi-faceted organization where relationships and responsibilities are more efficaciously demonstrated in the sharing of power.**

In Figure 1.2, Deal and Peterson (1991) noted five major foci of school reform for urban principals. With these major areas of concentration, it is quite obvious in today's large urban schools that one person can not effectively address each of these without sharing responsibilities, power, and decision-making. The roles of multi-leadership fit logically with these focus areas for urban school leadership and allow for a division and sharing of not only labor, but also expertise.

Figure 1.2

MAJOR FOCI	CKO	COO	CFO
Specific skills and needs of individuals involved in education	√		
The structure and operation of the school		√	
The political realities among the constituencies within the school	√	√	√
Educational economies involving choice and related markets			√
School culture	√	√	√

Murphy (2001) noted that with the dramatic changes in our world and in education, it is obvious that the principalship will need to be reconfigured as well. He offers four metaphors that capture the essence of the role of the principal in this 21st century:

- **Principal as Organizational Architect**: Today's new principal will need to learn—and help others to learn—about principles of postindustrial organizations, and assist teachers, students, and parents to reconstruct schools consistent with these principles.
- **Principal as Social Architect**: Schools in this new century are a major factor in the adequacy of the nation's response to the changing social fabric, and principals will have a larger role in determining whether the school's efforts are successful. Principals need to see education as one element of a larger attack on the problems facing at-risk children and give voice to the moral imperative to address these problems beyond the school. Also, this new principal will need to help design and construct an integrated network of social agencies to address the conditions confronting many students and their families. At the same time, the principal must also redesign the purpose and structure of the school to better serve its changing student population.

- **Principal as Educator**: These new leaders must provide students with more complex and demanding educational experiences than ever before. They must reach a large number of students who have not experienced success even under less demanding standards and expectations. To accomplish this, they will need to be more committed to educating children than ever before. This new principal will need to be broadly educated and more knowledgeable about teaching and learning.

- **Principal as Moral Agent**: In this new century, a major initiative appears to be forming to address the issue of values in education and to recognize the moral dimension of schooling in general and of the principalship in particular. At the core of this is an acknowledgement of the fact that value judgements are central in selecting and realizing educational goals. The principal's school activities are intertwined with critical and ethical issues. At a deeper level, the principalship is being slowly transformed into an instrument of social justice.

(p. 2-3)

Conclusion

The typical school building principal wears many *hats and shoes* in today's schools. Those in the role of administrator—building level principals—are levied undeniable accountability in the foundation, sustainability, and visionary demands for effective school reform initiatives. While traditions of K-12 educational leadership can have deep roots in the minds and hearts of public education's constituency, the prevailing educational *season* has brought challenges to the arena that demand a more critical appraisal of, "What is best for the children and young adults' in twenty-first century classrooms?" The call for the question is answered in this text with the Alston Model for Multi-leadership, which can help support effective leadership and undoubtedly contribute to student academic achievement.

Chapter 2

COO: The Principal as the Chief Operating Officer

It's 7:00 a.m. and the day has begun once again for Dr. Anita D. Robinson, principal of Beaseley High School. Dr. Robinson arrived in her office at 6:30 a.m. and began going through her morning routine before stepping out to begin her day as the principal of an inner city high school (circa 1975-capacity 1300) with an over enrollment of 1800 students. Along with the overcrowding of students, there are not enough certified teachers to cover all of the classes, so there are many permanent and daily subs, a lack of materials, student discipline issues, and the other daily grinds of running a school.

Introduction

The above scenario describes the beginning of a typical day for a principal of an urban high school. With these types of challenges, the principal is very task-oriented and focused on the order of the school, even before one student arrives, against unusual events (i.e., teacher absence, weather, facility mishaps, etc.) and day-to-day disturbances (Sergiovanni, Burlingame, Coombs and Thurston 1999). Correspondingly, in a multi- leadership model, the Chief Operating Officer of a company, is responsible for the day-to-day management of a business. This managerial role for a school administrator emerged in the mid-1800s as the building principal dealt mainly with routine maintenance activities and ensured that teachers and students adhered to building and district level policies (Sergiovanni et. al 1999). Contemporarily, in the context of the urban school, the principal does indeed function in this managerial capacity creating and maintaining a sense of order and discipline (Lightfoot 1983).

It is the daily and continual interaction with students and staff that takes the bulk of the principal's time. As a managerial job, the position of the COO consists of "an inner core of *demands*, an outer boundary of *constraints*, and an in-between area of *choices*" (Stewart 1982, 14). These demands are those things that the principal must do—things that are determined by school academic learning guidelines, legal requirements, bureaucratic rules and regulations, and the infinite idiosyncratic expectations of various constituencies. While the business model of management operates under a variety of constraints, the constraints that emerge as part of school operations are determined by the norms and values that exist in the district, availability of human and material resources, union contracts, space limitations, the capability/ limitations of teachers, the community at large and others with whom the principal must work (Sergiovanni 2001).

This chapter outlines the primary ways that this division of labor in the school leadership model, wherein the COO (Chief Operating Officer) enhances the building level efficiency at the organizational level with particular attention on culture and climate; student-related incidents; discipline; teachers and teacher organizations; classified staff; facilities; and policy.

Culture and Climate

Every school in every district across the nation manifests a cultural milieu that is uniquely its own. In addition to the daily demands that the COO undertakes, the person in this position is also primarily responsible for keeping abreast of the wellbeing of each school's distinct culture and climate.

Climate is defined as the "feeling that is conveyed in a group by the physical layout and the way in which members of the organization interact with each other, with customers, or with other outsiders" (Schein 1992, 2). Expanding that definition, Tagiuri (1968) noted that there are three elements of climate in an organization:

◆ Ecology – the physical elements of the facility;
◆ Milieu – the social dimension of the organization, including its demographic makeup, morale, and motivation;
◆ Social System – organizational and administrative structure.

(as cited in Marion 2002, 230)

A diverse culture and a healthy climate that is conducive to teaching and learning would be foundational if not critical in support of the Chief Knowledge Officer (CKO) to carry out the plans for the delivery of content area courses and extracurricular activities that support academic endeavors. This healthy climate is a climate wherein there is organization, whereby students (as well as teachers) take pride in what they do; teachers are teaching; a variety of teaching methodologies are being utilized; student and teachers are engaged and excited about the process; student work is displayed in ways that show a value for learner ownership in the knowledge acquisition process; and caregivers as well as community visitors are welcomed as partners in the education enterprise.

On the other hand, culture is defined as the "shared system of values and norms that define appropriate attitudes and behaviors for organizational members" (O'Reilly and Chatman 1996, 160). Sergiovanni (2001) noted the following regarding culture:

> Cultural life in schools is constructed reality, and school principals can play a key role in building this reality. School culture includes values, symbols, beliefs, and shared meanings of parents, students, teachers, and others conceived as a group or community. Culture governs what is worth for this group and how members should think, feel, and behave. The 'stuff' of culture includes a school's customs and traditions; historical accounts; stated and unstated understandings, habits, norms, and expectations; common meanings; and shared assumptions. The more understood, accepted, and cohesive the culture of a school, the better able it is to move in concert toward ideals it holds and objectives it wishes to pursue. (p. 105)

The COO as a cultural leader is one who has vision, mission, standards, and desires to build successful communities. It is in this community of practice (Drath and Palus 1994), that people are united by more than membership in a group [the school body], they are involved with one another in action [active participants in the educational process] (Lave and Wenger 1991).

S. (Simple) H. (Human) I. (Issues) T. (Today)

When the daily order of a building is disrupted, the COO will be called to quell all disturbances, so that the school may continue to run with fewer glitches, like a well-oiled machine. For instance, when students are in and out of the principal's office each day, this creates disruptions for teachers and other students. Many times, student and teacher friction is often at the root of many office-referred infractions. Student allegations of being treated unfairly must be investigated, and teachers must feel supported as they endeavor to deliver content related instruction daily without disruption to the pedagogical process. In response the COO should be responsible for the development of a discipline plan that involves professional development to help teachers and students with conflict resolution and culturally related models of intervention. Most often student-initiated disturbances, depending on the severity are dealt with on a case-by-case basis. One may disperse student arguments in the hallway, sending students on their way. Other times it may require the disciplinary procedures of the school/district to be enacted. In either case, if a typical principal dealing with what can be mundane hallway logistics or the recipe for an assault, either procedure takes time away from dealing with instructional issues. When the principal is called upon to deal with disturbances the focus is taken from routine pedagogy and ancillary things related to community, school enhancement, or enrichment.

While the CKO is left to undertake instructional issues with a greater priority, the COO (in a multi-leadership model), while still involved in the daily workings of the school, would have more time to handle operational situations, often giving top priority to day-to-day, hour-to hour, minute-to minute, disturbances related to a discipline plan. This discipline plan must require the commitment of all adults in the school. As team members of the principalship, the CKO and the COO along with teachers must share in the authority while carrying out the plan; students, too, must have some sense of ownership in this plan (Meyers and Pawlas 1989). The COO, for instance, may lay as a foundation the eight factors associated with schools and good discipline:

1.   the way people work to solve problems;
2.   the way authority and status are allocated and symbolized in the school;
3.   the degree to which students feel they belong in the school and feel that it serves them;

4. the way rules are developed, communicated and enforced;
5. the ways of dealing with personal problems of students and staff;
6. the way in which the physical facility and the organizational structure of the school reinforce educational goals;
7. the relationship between the school community and the home it serves; and
8. the quality of the curriculum and the instructional practice.

(Phi Delta Kappa 1982)

In addition to the teachers, students, staff, and community, these eight factors would require the complete support and coordination of the leadership team with each member, the CKO, the COO, and the CFO involved in the effective and efficient administration of discipline policy.

Disturbances to the school day, however, are to be expected; it should not be an expectation for these disturbances to impede school order. The COO should be visibly interacting with all constituency groups, not one who sits in the office but rather be an active building manager. This individual must deal with district level edicts, order supplies, keep hallways and playgrounds safe, put out fires that threaten tranquil public relations and make sure the busing and meal services are operating smoothly (IEL 2000).

Discipline

Discipline can be training, punishment, and a means for maintaining control. Some issues regarding school discipline go beyond the "S. (simple) H. (human) I. (issues) T. (today)" that happen in the daily classroom or schoolyard management; these may involve serious acts of violence, gang activity, racial conflict, and bomb threats that may necessitate suspension or expulsion when individual students are found to be at fault. Schools are a microcosm of the world in which we live. Drake and Roe (2003) posited, "discipline should be considered one of the most meaningful learning experiences in the school. In the broadest sense, it involves learning to adjust and cope successfully with society and to relate positively with other people of various ages, intelligence, and backgrounds" (p. 412).

Current events related to school safety and security (increasing numbers of school related deaths—Columbine, Jonesboro, W. Paducah) and an international agenda with heightened focus on violence in our world, also presents school personnel daily challenges giving safety and security the highest priority. Students deserve the right to come to schools that offer maximum opportunities for academic achievement but also maintain safe zones. While security breaches that require lockdown procedures, the initiation and implementation of policy to deal with the reporting of student/student and student/teacher assaults, keeping school weapon-free zones, stopping the destruction of school and personal property and cross-cultural conflict may all be very important, the COO acts in a role of educational leadership with specificity to the operation of the building. The ways that the Chief Operating Officer can exert leadership with regard to violence include the following:

- Reviewing and or establishing uniform disciplinary practices known by students, teachers, parents, and school board members;
- Involving as many adults in the school as possible;
- Meeting problems early and openly;
- Visiting in the community and enlisting the help of neighbors to monitor the school area for unusual or destructive behavior;
- Planning with custodial and maintenance staff regarding opportunities they may have to help instill pride in the facilities, effect rapid repairs and cleaning, suggest materials to elevate potential problems;
- Establish a liaison with police officials to agree on when police should be called and how such incidents will be handled for the proper protection of all;
- Develop a plan to keep weapons out of school; and
- Providing in-service education to faculty and staff on how to deal with fights, violent parents, unknown intruders, and even organized gang activity.

(Drake and Roe 2003, 383)

Teachers and Teacher Organizations

Often a traditional principal is called upon to referee issues such as the following: scheduling conflicts; conflicts with classified staff and other paraprofessionals; issues of support with caregivers; financial support for teacher-related initiatives; clubs/new programs; teacher-to-teacher conflicts; assignments of bus duty, hall duty, lunch room duty; and parking. Differences in the perception of student and teacher conflict, teacher's lack of consistency, issues dealing with perceptions of what is *just* rather than *fair* often emerge when the principal must make a decision for the greater good of the school community rather than individual teacher needs.

Teacher organizations, most often in the form of teachers' unions, can maintain an adversarial role with the principal. Often, they are organized in levels of leadership that are in stark contrast to schools. For example a building representative (elected) is in contact with district level elected representatives, who are in turn in contact with state and national level delegates. Often there is a pattern of administration that must be followed and respected in dealing with any teacher-related issues regarding the perceptions or actual violation of district negotiated contracts. While this is not the case with all districts, it is the case with districts where the union representative is the first to know that a problem exists with administration and takes on an adversarial problem-solving role. The COO in this setting could develop relationships with teachers and teacher organizations in more in-depth ways that would facilitate the (re)creation of administration as an advocate for teachers rather than an antagonist.

Another area of great concern in urban settings is teacher attrition. Many urban schools for example begin each day with short and long-term substitutes. While instructionally this would come under the purview of the CKO, the COO would be faced with the issue of achieving a semblance of order each day as the faces of the school personnel, in this case, teachers, may change daily. When this lack of stability related to teacher personnel is present, the "routines of a building," are difficult to balance against the reality that the inconsistencies in pedagogy may create.

Facilities, Classified Staff, Transportation

Under this model of multi-leadership, the COO would be responsible for plant management, transportation, goods and custodial services, secretaries, and other classified staff (Pierce 2000). There should be an adequate number of janitorial staff, food service workers, and food services to meet the daily and emergency needs. All of these pieces help to provide an optimum climate for instruction.

The principal plays a key role in the planning and operation of the school facility (Drake and Roe 2003). This individual is charged with maintaining relationships with central office patterns of administration to deal with red tape related to "fixing" things inside and outside the building. The building should be in working order, have proper lighting, and be clean. Quite often, school visitors are quick to form corollary impressions about how the buildings and grounds are kept with judgments of a principal's leadership and students' academic success (Lipham, Rankin, and Hoeh 1985). Beyond the daily use of the building by students, faculty, staff, and administration, the building may also be used by the community and/or other agencies, such as religious organizations and/or civic clubs. Many schools, particularly those in urban areas, are serving as "one stop shopping" with regards to social services, continuing education, and recreation (full-service and community-in-schools). Drake and Roe (2003) noted that there should be clear procedures regarding the use of the building by community groups and other agencies. They suggest a checklist to use for extending the use of the available facilities:

1. What written policies are available regarding the use of the school buildings?
2. Who gives final approval? What routing is specified?
3. What steps are necessary to initiate requests? What forms?
4. How are charges determined?
5. What arrangements must be made for custodial services?
6. What community services should be notified (e.g., police, security patrol)? What are the appropriate procedures for this?
7. How much time should be allowed for each step and for the total request-approval process?
8. What measures should be taken with the faculty regarding the use of the building by community groups?
9. If the building can be scheduled by someone other than the principal, services coordinator, or administrative assistant, what safeguards exist to avoid scheduling conflicts?

(p. 476-477)

This extended use of school facilities after hours, weekends, and year round adds to the maintenance schedule and burden on the custodial team. While additional staffing to the facilities team would relieve the burden of additional work beyond the school and contractual day, the COO's relationship with the team would facilitate a sense of shared pride in the aspects of the building order that is related to a clean, operative, facility.

Often in teacher and administrative preparation programs it is said that two of the first people that you should become acquainted and maintain amenable contacts with are the secretary and the custodian. The traditional secretary has often been replaced by a team of clerical workers that are responsible for various aspects of the school office. The attendance records, the ordering of lunches, the answering of telephones, the word processing, the ordering of supplies and the meeting and greeting of visitors to the building are a few tasks that fall on the shoulders of the clerical or classified staff. This relationship—the COO and the classified staff—is imperative to the smooth running order in the building. The "buck" may stop at the desk of the administrator but it must pass the desk(s) of those who are often at the "front line" in many school offices. It may be that the traditional ways in which clerical and administrative paperwork is handled must also be revisited and given a multi-level model consideration for increased efficiency.

If the COO, the CKO, and the CFO were all given support staff that demonstrated the specificity related to each administrator's field of expertise and responsibility in the building, we could find that reports, for example, may be compiled in a more timely manner and the capacity to increase a school and district's ability to engage in more data-based decision making could be augmented. One area of informed data-based decision-making that must be given the attention daily in every school building is that of transportation.

The movement of students from their neighborhoods to the school is the single largest enterprise of transportation for many cities. This is especially the case for urban centers where public transportation may be used in addition to school busses. Busing related to school athletic events and extracurricular activities can present the traditional principal with many hours of waiting, negotiating, and paper work.

Implementation and Maintenance of School Policy

At the core of many school days is the maintenance and implementation of new policies that come from central office administration. From zero-tolerance policies to budget and attendance reports, the principal is often the single person interpreting, planing and executing district policy, and the single person in the position of accountability to their immediate supervisor, and ultimately the superintendent. For instance, if a student is found with anything that can be fashioned as a weapon, there is immediate suspension with a scheduled expulsion hearing. In a large high school the principal could find him or herself in hearing after hearing after hearing if the implementation of this policy finds its way into a school that is confronting an increase in gang activity. Each time the principal is out of the building some of the other responsibilities may be handled by an assistant principal or a teacher leader; however, there are some duties that can not be delegated and so tasks sit and wait, and often pile up waiting for the principal to return. In the Alston Model of Multi-leadership (see Fig. 1.1), the COO would be in a position to not only attend meetings that discuss the creation and procedures for implementation of policy, but would also be charged with that responsibility in the building.

Often school related policy making at the local, state, and federal level is lacking the essential voice of building administrators due to the time commitment that would pull the administrator from the building. The COO could, for example, attend meetings with local law enforcement and juvenile detention center education providers (often teachers) to help with the forging of partnerships that could facilitate more seamless delivery of education for juvenile offenders and to ensure that students rights and responsibilities are not violated.

Conclusion

Much like a ship's navigator with constant monitoring that steadies a course, the COO is daily monitoring and readjusting operationally to ensure that everyone reaches the destination—*academic success for all students.* Often student/teacher and student/student interactions, reports and documentation, Parent Teacher Association (PTA), caregiver and community advisory groups, and Boards of Education all require attention before during and after the regular school day. For example, when the community is supportive of the school/district agenda and welcomed as volunteers in areas of academic support then the partnerships forged often mediate a perception of effective leadership and academic achievement. When the politics of a district or some media splash of a particular school incident cast the school/district in a disparaging light then the challenge of maintaining good public relations is complex. In dealing with this, the COO needs to have strong (influential) and effective communication skills to deal with the press, keep the school running effectively and to suppress the onset of internal melancholy and outside negative influences that may interrupt the preservation of a conducive learning environment.

In traditional models of school administrative leadership, one person is expected to be in two or three places at once, to be aware of every operational matter in the building and be responsible for trouble shooting effectively in each of these situations. Often, just the physical impossibility of the traditional model is evidenced in the many situations that can only be reacted to rather than detected early as challenges, so that creative plans for intervention may be proposed and successful implementation realized. A multi-leadership model could support a pattern of administration that creates a space where one member of the administrative team, the COO is given the latitude of specificity in regards to building operations and the "luxury" of time for more reflective and purposeful implementation.

Chapter 3

CFO: The Principal as the Chief Financial Officer

For proficient principals, sound fiscal management begins with the establishment of program goals and objectives. In fiscal management, the proficient principal:

♦ Understands the school district budget and its implications for the school;

♦ Involves members of the school community in developing budget priorities based on the mission and goals of the school; and

♦ Prepares the school budget in accordance with school district budgeting procedures. (Sergiovanni 2001, 6)

Introduction

Fiscal stewardship is one of the obligations of the principal. In accordance with Sergiovanni's above description of fiscal management at the school level, the principal as CFO (Chief Financial Officer) would be in charge of budgets, as well as grants, fundraising, and establishing a school endowment fund to raise money for enrichment, expanded content area programming, books, and other items. This expansion in line items for the school budget would represent additions to what is provided in the general fund at the building level through allocation at central office administration. This individual, the CFO, is responsible for translating the educational goals and objectives into specific budgetary requests, preparing and defending the school's budget, monitoring the use of resources provided, and evaluating educational outcomes in programmatic terms (Lipham, Rankin, and Hoeh 1985).

Considerations of equity in school funding are embedded in the history related to the financing of public education. Urban schools since their inception have been plagued with inadequate and misappropriated funding. Teachers and students in these schools have consistently faced a scarcity (and often inequitable allocation) of resources (Weiner 1999, 14). Weiner continued, "in most urban school districts, administrators at the school level have remarkably little power to make significant changes in the school's operations" (p. 41). The various formulas for the dispersal of funds on the state and local level have been fodder for the courts across this nation. As the United States becomes increasingly fragmented by wealth, equity continues to be an important issue (Sergiovanni 1999), particularly in the discussion of public school funding. There is a relationship between adequate financial resources, student achievement and educational gains. For example, the teacher to student ratio is often a contractual item, but personnel budgets determine the number of teachers that can be hired. While there are arguments in the academic and research arenas regarding whether or not that relationship (low teacher to student ratio) is positive or negative, many children (particularly those in urban areas) are not given the opportunity to participate in the "laboratory classroom" due to the cost of pilot programs. **All students have a right to the quality education that adequate resources can provide.**

A discussion of what constitutes *quality* education would be apropos here. Often the allocation of resources is a discussion of personnel and supplies. However, inadequate facilities (discussed in Chapter 2) are also a part of the disparity in urban public schools. While a lack of a quality education may mean students not having access to higher level classes (i.e., advanced placement), a discussion of how to fix a leaking roof and adequately heat classrooms is corollary to the poorest schools receiving the lowest appropriation of fiscal resources. Does money does make a difference? Until each school has all the fiscal resources it needs, and every school is equitably funded, will we be able to say yes or no to that question. The CFO, giving fiscal matters the highest priority, would endeavor to plan and implement fiscal reform efforts that directly impact student academic achievement.

With this information in mind, it is clear that at the building level, it is imperative to have one individual who will focus on not only fiscal responsibility with the allocated general fund budget, but also one who must pursue and secure external funding to enhance and enrich school initiatives. For instance, research in experiential student learning supports that many students should have as many experiences outside the classroom as possible for authentic application of concepts and theories developed in traditional classroom learning contexts. These experiences (study abroad programs, field-based internships, etc.) often encumber financial obligations that far exceed the urban or rural student's ability to individually pay or his or her school's ability to offer financial support. A CFO whose priority is more than just keeping the school's finances in the "black" would also seek grant writing and development opportunities that would augment the curricular and content area learning outcomes and simultaneously enrich the learning opportunities for students.

In addition to financial responsibilities, the CFO also has liability for the business-related management of the school. Thus, this individual is responsible "for the traditional business functions of accountability, purchase requisitions, and materials management, but also these are expanded in scope, and in some instances, personnel budgets and/or energy management are a part of the building administrator's responsibilities" (Drake and Roe 2003, 453). In FY 2001 over 340 billion dollars were spent to educate public elementary and secondary school students in the United States (*Digest of Education Statistics* 2002). Once appropriated as a federal expenditure to the district and then to individual schools, the size of many building level budgets coupled with the specificity of school budgetary policy, the administrator who undertakes the role of the CFO should have school finance experience and business management expertise. Many urban school districts can no longer *afford* to find themselves in squandered and mismanaged already scarce resources. The recovery from a loss of public trust could mean a loss in the elective franchise when a school levy is on the ballot at best and procurement by the state due to mismanagement with funding at worse.

School Budget External Funding

Present budgetary practices are the result of a long evolutionary development, which has recently been accelerating rather than stabilizing or decelerating. The traditional principles and practices of budgeting, which seemed to be well established and proven, are now being supplanted or supplemented by more sophisticated systems of interpreting the educational program of the school. (Burrup, Brimley, and Garfield 1999, 279)

The school budgetary process involves planning the budget, preparing the budget, managing the budget, and evaluating the budget (Frohreich, 1983). Additional monies in the financial portion of the Alston Model of Multi-leadership (see Fig. 1.1) include grants, fundraising, school endowment, and corporate partnerships. The idea of budgeting fiscal allocations implies conceptually the control of expenditures. However, with high stakes accountability and the pressure to raise levels of proficiency, we see an increasing wave of fiscal rewards earmarked for principals and teachers when scores on standardized measures of achievement are met. This creates a fiscal differential between teachers and administrators within districts. The multi-leadership model's CFO, in concert with the CKO could provide a shared vision for the type of supports needed to increase test scores. While these initiatives may be costly on the front end, the investment would yield future revenue to the building as a building moves from academic emergency, for example, to academic excellence.

(Mis)Management

Unfortunately, empirical data support the assumptions that often the levels of waste and mismanagement of school funds is due to negligence at best and criminal activity at worst. Loose policies that govern the handling of school money can often present either innocent or intentional mishandling of money from school-sponsored activities. While media coverage of school embezzlement is rare, it is all too common to hear of the dismissal of a principal or school treasurer under a shroud of controversy. For example, in one large mid-western urban public school district the treasurer was asked to resign and upon his refusal, was fired when capital funds were unaccounted for after a district level audit. In this same school district a principal was put on administrative leave without pay, indicted, prosecuted, and terminated for inappropriately using monies from building level funds for a retirement party. Clearly, the context of each district's fiscal circumstances may vary, but the accountability and responsibility for frugality is a shared dilemma.

"Money —or the lack of it—will govern the way an organization is managed and the way it succeeds" (Drake and Roe 2003, 455). Sound fiscal management procedures can prevent mismanagement from occurring (Walter and Marconnit 1989). The CFO (along with the Business Manager/Financial Specialist [see Fig. 1.1]) would also be responsible for training others in the school in the proper procedures for handling all school funds (bake sales, senior shirt sales, petty cash, booster clubs, athletic events, etc.). The CFO must first establish a clear set of guidelines regarding the handling of building funds, and these guidelines must be consistent with state accounting and auditing procedures. Walter and Marconnit (1989) suggested the following basic (commonsensical) items to be included in such guidelines:

> ➢ In school-related business, no transaction should be made in cash, except for those small amounts disbursed from a petty cash fund. By using checks for all disbursements, the school has a record of the transaction for accounting purposes. The CFO and Financial/Business Specialist also should encourage school patrons to use checks or money orders as a standard practice when paying for tickets and other items sold by the school. Checks and money orders provide a record of payment; cash does not.

> ➢ The school district should secure a blanket bond for all employees who handle money. Bonding is relatively inexpensive and provides an additional safeguard for the school. The bonding company assumes the liability should funds be found missing or stolen and is responsible for seeing that dishonest employees make restitution.

> ➢ Never use personal checking accounts as depositories for monies collected at school. Give monies collected to the CFO, obtain a receipt, and the CFO will record the amount in the appropriate activity account. Even classroom book-club purchases should go through the office. The CFO/CFO-designate should set up a special book-club account. When an order is ready to be sent; the CFO can prepare a school check and include it with the order.

> ➢ Activity sponsors should turn over monies collected to the CFO for deposit in the bank as soon as possible. Activity funds should not be left over-night in a teacher's desk or classroom closet, nor should they be taken home. Monies collected at night activities can be dropped in your banks' night depository.

> ➢ Students and staff should not make cash purchases for school items from personal funds and then request reimbursement from the school activity fund. Instead, they should charge the items after clearance from the CFO, CFO-designate, or sponsor.

> ➢ When depositing money with the CFO, a sponsor or student should count it, fill out a deposit slip, and get a receipt.

> ➢ A prudent policy is to have all checks signed by two persons. Thus no one person has the sole authority to authorize checks or to withdraw funds from school accounts.

> ➢ When merchandise for a school activity is ordered and will be delivered at a later date, a Payment Authorization Voucher form should be used.

There is an old saying, " Too many cooks in the kitchen can spoil the soup." Often at the building level the mismanagement of school funds is not due to the deliberate criminal intent of a teacher as a booster club faculty advisor or the principal "skimming" money from the ticket sales of a weekly basketball game. Instead it is usually due to someone forgetting money in a drawer, to receipts not being kept, or several people "helping" with fundraising events' proceeds. To avoid mismanagement, it is advisable to have clearly adopted (where there exists no district level policy) in the form of school-based policy regarding how all fluid assets and liabilities will be handled. This is not to suggest that some teachers and other school-based personnel are not capable of handling expenditures. Many of them are very capable and have year in and year out, volunteered, in addition to their teaching, counseling or coaching responsibilities to assist with fiscal administrative duties. The point of a multi-leadership model, however, allows those very capable teachers to do just what the students and community depend on them to do—teach. Leaving what is often labeled as "administrivia" to one person supports a structure of uniformity that would allow for the accountability to be more stringent. This would also allow the COO and the CFO to monitor closely the fiscal year allocation and expenditures before a problem may arise.

A multi-leadership model will not eliminate all the challenges that schools and districts face with funds. Since the dawn of private and public schooling in America there have been challenges with school spending from centralized appropriated resources to decentralized responsibility based budgets. **Choosing a model of multi-leadership (implemented in some manner) that shifts the weight of fiscal responsibilities from a single person with many other contractual obligations (i.e., a traditional principal) to a one person with specific functions (i.e., the CKO) is sound in these times of increased school fiscal and academic accountability.** No one would expect a pitcher of a baseball team to cover all the bases, the left, right, and center field as well as protect home base. We have for too long expected one person as the administrative leader in a school to do just that. If the CFO in the building can be relied on to uniformly handle the fiscal matters of each individual school's budgetary circumstance and monitor the impact that each fiscal endeavor will have on the entire school budget, then urban schools could find that some of the challenges related to fiscal details would diminish.

Decentralization/Site-Based Fiscal Management

> The bottom line is that school based management is not an end in itself, although research indicates that it can help foster an improved school culture and higher quality decisions. School based management is, however, a potentially valuable tool for engaging the talents and enthusiasm of far more of school's stakeholders than traditional, top-down governance systems. Moreover, once in place, school based management holds the promise of enabling schools to better address students' needs. (Wohlstetter and Mohrman 1994, 1)

American education is being paralyzed by a hierarchical bureaucracy (Sizer 1985). Furthermore, Sizer stated "the structure is getting in the way of children's learning" (p. 206). One response to this is School-based Decision-making (SBM), which has been very well received in public education. It is founded on the premise that the school is the fundamental decision-making unit within the education system and that its administrators, teachers, and other professional support staff constitute a natural decision-making and management team. Each school is essentially an autonomous unit with the principal in the role of Chief Executive Officer (Razik and Swanson 2001). Here the emphasis is on results. The teachers and administrators in the school are responsible for establishing goals that focus on student outcomes, communicating those goals to students and parents, and deciding how to produce the results they seek (Oswald 1995).

Conclusion

In these times of school financial reform on the federal, state, and local levels and the increasing systemic levels of checks and balances, the traditional principal is found taking many hours from other important aspects of leadership to deal with fiscal procedures that must be in place, so that school monies are properly accounted for (Walter and Marconnit 1989). The CFO in the Alston Model of Multi-leadership can give attention to budgets and reports on various expenditures as requested by the district, and oversee the requisitioning and allocation of supplies at the building level. In many budgetary models, for example, there is per pupil expenditure given to each school in a district based on attendance reports compiled on by a given date. The CFO working closely with the COO would have more accurate data to report to the district regarding attendance, thereby possibly increasing the allocations to a given school when attendance reporting is left to often overworked school clerical support staff.

As district level school budgets become tighter, ergo, building level budgets, many principals attempt to meet this challenge with increased involvement in public relations and fundraising to secure financial support for their schools from local businesses and the community (*Occupational Outlook Handbook* 2002). Too often, the public is confused when as taxpayers they are requested to approve a levy ballot for operating monies for schools that are often touted in the media as failing at the educational enterprise. The constituencies that make up the tax base want schools without academic failure and demand increased fiscal responsibility for existing state and local budgets. Often the public's response to low academic achievement is a clamor for increased budget accountability. In some states, the legislative response to voters' outcries has been support for privatization (vouchers) and charter schools. The CFO, as a part of an administrative team, could become an advocate for urban public schools by lobbying for educating voters as it relates to financial matters while simultaneously sharing the ways that this restructuring of school leadership supports accountablity for how money is actually spent.

Chapter 4:

CKO: The Principal as the Chief Knowledge Officer

Learning doesn't happen without leadership.
(Institute for Educational Leadership 2000, 2)

Introduction

In a business model, the Chief Knowledge Officer (CKO) is the corporate executive in charge of structuring a company's store of technical and business knowledge, and ensuring that employees have access to that knowledge (Logophilia Limited 1998). Neilson (2001) suggested that the role of the CKO in a public sector organization revolves around ten areas:

- ➤ Provide leadership and strategy
- ➤ Measure outcomes
- ➤ Promote "best" practices and processes
- ➤ Create knowledge-sharing culture
- ➤ Champion communities of practice
- ➤ Use incentives and rewards
- ➤ Provide tools and technology
- ➤ Champion education

> Create and use taxonomy (common language)
> Secure resources

Correspondingly, under the Alston Model of Multi-leadership (see Fig. 1.1), the Chief Knowledge Officer (CKO) along with an instructional specialist become the individuals responsible for instructional leadership, and like Neilson's (2001) model, the role of the CKO in a school would follow the similar paths. The CKO as instructional leader much like the CKO in the public sector organization will "promote best practices and processes." As the CKO, for instance, collects data on successful teacher preparation programs for urban centers, the benchmarks for interviewing teachers to fill empty teaching positions in an urban school may be situated in looking for prospective teacher candidates with qualifications that correlate with competencies that "best practices" data support. This change in the infrastructure as it relates to interviewing can contribute to the hiring of teachers in urban centers that may be more successful initially and over time.

A building principal has many duties each hour of each day. Often two major tasks of the administrator are neglected at best and ignored at worst. The first (no hierarchy implied) of these major tasks is working toward the improvement peculiar to the quality of life for each individual within the school; the second is the exercising of leadership in order to make a positive difference in student learning–instructional leadership (Drake and Roe 2003).

What Is Instructional Leadership?

Instructional leadership can be defined in different ways. Ching-Jen Liu (as cited in Daresh 2002) provided a succinct definition, in stating that "instructional leadership consists of direct or indirect behaviors that significantly affect teacher instruction and as a result, student learning" (p. 108). Research has suggested that in order to create and maintain effective schools, the principal must be actively engaged in instructional leadership. Thus, it has been widely agreed upon that a principal's primary concern should be his or her role as instructional leader (Boyd 1996).

However, this may not happen in urban settings because of the many other equally important issues that principals must deal with first before getting to the instruction and supervision of teachers (Sanders 1999). What are some reasons that these principals don't exercise more instructional leadership? Buffie (1989) suggested several reasons:

1. They tend to allocate their time according to the priorities established by the central office administration.
2. While they may accept the importance of instructional leadership, they often do not know how to proceed.
3. Neither their professional preparation nor in-service programs have been oriented toward developing instructional leadership skills.
4. Demands of administrative–managerial tasks consume almost all of their time and attention.
5. It is much easier to be an administrator/manager than it is to be an instructional leader. (p. 3)

Hallinger and Murphy (1987) argued that the district level leadership must reduce obstacles that inhibit building principals from completing their instructional leadership tasks. These tasks include: leadership and instructional goals, leadership and curriculum content, leadership and organizing curriculum experiences for learning, leadership and the improvement of instructional programming, leadership and the evaluation of school performance, and maintaining an orderly climate (Kimbrough and Burkett 1990). Thus, instructional leadership presents challenges on many levels.

The Instructional Leadership Challenge

Instructional leadership involves taking risks, managing others, collaborating, and being held accountable. The instructional leader's role is of one of great importance for several reasons. First, effective instructional leadership has been linked to positive student outcomes. Short and Spencer (1990) found that "effective principals' instructional leadership was related to student's positive perceptions of their classroom environment and social climate" (p. 120). Andrews and Soder (1987) agreed that the principal's role in instructional leadership is critical in improving the outcomes of students. The literature suggests several models for increasing the principal's role as instructional leader. One model theorizes that principals would become instructional leaders by teaching one class a day. Boyd (1996) asserted that "it gives the principal a continuous feel for the educational process, allows for the testing of administrative decisions or policy, serves as a source of ideas, provides for direct access between principals and students, and keeps the principal active in an academic discipline" (p. 69). Another model suggested by Dukes (as cited in Hoerr 1996) explained that "instructional leadership includes four relevant areas that principals must address: teacher supervision, teacher evaluation, staff development, and quality control" (p. 104). Furthermore, another suggestion is based on simple communication and collaboration with staff. From this nucleus would come strategies and plans for school-wide improvement (Hoerr 1996). **No matter what the model, plan, or suggestion, it clear that there is a strong need for instructional leadership.** Instructional leadership is a component of effective educational administration and supervision. Hopefully, the principal who asserts himself or herself as a strong instructional leader will have a positive impact on teachers, students, and academic outcomes. In the process, teachers would recognize the principal's interest and dedication to support pedagogically sound learning communities. Students, in turn, would realize the principal as CKO is genuinely invested in their academic success. Whitaker (1997) affirmed that effective instructional leaders understand that the truly important activities in a school take place in the classrooms, and that these leaders have a stake in the learning process. Finally, effective instructional leaders can collaborate with all school personnel to create and support a school culture that fosters students reaching the highest levels of academic success. Fasion, Smith, and Andrews (as cited in Boyd 1996) found that "effective and high-achieving schools...depend most on capable instructional leadership from principals" (p. 66). Therefore, the principal's role as instructional leader becomes paramount.

Requisite Skills of the CKO

In this educational atmosphere of accountability and choice, (school vouchers or charter schools), instructional leadership is requisite for the survival and success of today's urban schools. Edmonds (as cited in Whitaker 1997) suggested "the principal has to be the person the instructional personnel look to for instructional leadership in the system. If they do not, the implications for the school are considerably negative" (p. 155). In the midst of numerous pressures such as standardized methods of assessment, media exaggeration and propagandizing, and outcome-based assessments, the necessity for instructional leadership unfolds. Gainey (1993) maintained that "it is not a question of whether or not principals can be instructional leaders, they *must* be instructional leaders" (p. 57). These leaders must be people-oriented and interactional, as well as have good networking skills and mentoring ability (Whitaker 1997). In essence, the CKO must be a visible collegial force in the school, stay abreast of curricular issues and changes, and model appropriate behaviors for teachers in reference to teaching and learning (Ash and Persall 2000). Often urban districts find that the teaching force is *young*–with many of the teachers in classrooms having less than five years of experience. Urban school sites not only have a young teaching force, but also are often not able to retain teachers, losing many of them their third year of service. A CKO, as instructional leader, would be able to work closely with these teachers many of whom experience difficulty with discipline and instructional strategies in the classroom. The CKO could also tailor professional development for all teachers in general. However, there should be a focus on new teachers, in particular, that would highlight areas that need improvement as well as provide them with needed support. At the same time, the CKO must also set an instructional agenda for the school and maintain effective communication among various groups. With this in mind, Patterson (1993) suggested that instructional leaders engage in participative management (shared decision-making), provide support for and monitor instruction, are resourceful, and most importantly provide a sense of vision for their schools. Including this concept of vision, Buffie (1989) noted that there are six other key skills that an instructional leader needs to possess: communicating, developing trust, motivating others, decision-making, planning, and promoting collegiality.

Vision

The instructional agenda is the CKO's vision for the school in reference to academics. Kouzes and Posner (1995) defined vision as "an ideal and unique image of the future" (p. 95). Therefore, the instructional agenda of the CKO should be one that sets a standard of excellence and at the same time be exceptional enough to avoid the growing trend of lowering the bar to only meet baseline academic skills. In addition, this vision could be a framework that could allow for additional input. Sergiovanni (1995) noted:

> Vision is an important dimension of purposing and without it the very point of leadership is missed, but the vision of the school must reflect the hopes and dreams, the needs and interests, the values and beliefs of everyone who has a stake in the school. (p. 132)

Generally, the local, state, and national agendas, often communicated in the form of standards, leave teachers feeling overwhelmed and confused. The CKO's responsibility would be to synthesize these multiple agendas, integrate the needs of the district and the needs of the individual school with a community perspective and create sagacity for instruction. This is no easy task. The CKO must be in tune to multiple agendas and much like a master sculptor, chiseling away at what is unnecessary to work toward the realization of the finished product. The finished products in this case are students who are not only able to demonstrate the acquisition of academic concepts, but who will also soon contribute in participatory ways as adults in their communities in general and society at large. This emphasizes the importance of a shared vision. This is not to suggest that every decision of the CKO will be made in collaboration with others as it relates to instruction. It does posit, however, that the role of leader in the arena of instruction can best facilitate the implementation of a mission, and a vision that is responsive and progressive in the educational endeavor. An important element in creating and maintaining a shared vision is fostering effective communication, which is another important talent of the CKO.

Communication

Communication is an important aspect of building community (Sergiovanni 2001). In order for the CKO to be effective, communication is crucial. Open lines of communication can help the CKO create the kind of organizational infrastructure needed to impact positive change. How can the CKO foster effective communication? First, this individual must be highly visible. This includes visiting classrooms and talking and listening to teachers (Ash and Persall 2000). Visibility could also include attendance at after-school functions, professional development opportunities often intended *just for teachers*, state and national conferences, the teacher's lounge, and the infamous parking lot conversations. The key here is that the CKO is readily available and easily accessible to those who are most often during the school day not in the office areas.

Secondly, the CKO should provide opportunities for feedback. This could be done through a number of methods such as suggestion boxes, listproc discussions, and informal surveys (Kouzes and Posner 1995). While the need for direct and specific feedback is important, opportunities for teachers and staff to learn what constitutes feedback is also important. Many times school personnel welcome the opportunity to just "get something off his/her chest." While this may help the individual feel better, it does not always provide for the organization, in this case the CKO or other administrators what necessary feedback is needed to assess exactly what a problem is, propose solutions, and if necessary allocate resources to make a change. For example, a science teacher or a team of teachers may in every staff meeting complain that the science laboratory conditions are deplorable, and that the level of scientific experimentation they would like to conduct is impossible in the labs. This may allow them to "let off some steam" and receive validation that their assessment is correct. But, when these same teachers are given training in how to give feedback, their responses may change to: "If we are to teach the student learning outcomes found in the 7th grade curriculum guide, then the science lab is in need of 3 working Bunsen burners, 4 student work stations, 250 test tubes, 15 pairs of safety glasses and a better ventilation system." The CKO with this *feedback* in the form of a request for equipment correlated to student learning outcomes is able to meet with the CFO and investigate the resources available in order to make decisions that would support instructional delivery and student achievement.

Thirdly, the CKO should promote some type of outreach program aimed at community members, parents, and caregivers. One effective tool for outreach is a newsletter. Newsletters can now be distributed with little cost when made available electronically on district maintained web pages. In addition, town hall meetings could be held to keep individuals aware of academic changes and challenges, instructional strategies, and success stories. More often than not, community members, parents and caregivers have predetermined ideas about the schools in their neighborhoods. These perceptions may or may not be true. What is a public "truth" are the test scores of students from a particular school or school district. The CKO must work to develop a level of communication that facilitates open lines of communication so that more than a "single snapshot" (i.e., standardized test scores) of a given school becomes the prevailing narrative. This means that a level of reciprocal trust must be attained as Cox (1993) asserted–**healthy communication can build trust.**

Trust /Collegiality

The Merriam-Webster Dictionary (Woolf 1974) defined trust as (1) assured reliance on the character, strength, or truth of someone or something; (2) a basis of reliance, faith, or hope; and (3) something entrusted to one to be cared for in the interest of another. Buffie (1989) defined trust as the emotional glue that binds followers and leaders and as the basic ingredient in all effective organizations. Additionally, Bredeson (1989) commented that principals desire to be seen by parents as approachable, fair, honest, and empathetic. This individual–at *all* levels of the multi-leadership model, want to create and sustain a culture and climate where trust is at the nucleus of all relationships. The principal as CKO has been charged with leading the effort for the educational wellbeing of the students in his or her building. Each day parents and caregivers send their children to schools in response to the unspoken agreement that teachers will teach and administrators will maintain a climate conducive to teaching and learning. When this trust is broken, parents who are in privileged positions *vote with their feet* and opt for private or parochial schools. Families that are economically fragile are often disenchanted and disenfranchised and thus may not fully participate in their child's education. **Parent support of the schooling process is a non-negotiable element for student success.** Community members, parents, and caregivers who trust school personnel are more likely to extend their support. Therefore, trust is fundamental for this individual's success in this position.

The CKO must also develop a relationship of trust and collegiality with teachers, classified staff and other school personnel. Because the CKO can not, for instance, be in every classroom at all times, teaching every lesson, he or she must trust and support the teachers who are there to deliver education to the students. Trust in teachers' ability and professionalism will lead to teacher empowerment—the CKO trusts that many teachers are capable of leadership and choose the classroom. The CKO along with input from these teachers will make the best decisions regarding the welfare and achievement of students entrusted to their care on a daily basis.

When speaking of trust, one also speaks of moral and ethical leadership. Standard Five of the Interstate School Leaders Licensure Consortium (see Chapter 5) clearly states that a school administrator is an educational leader who promotes the success of all students by acting with integrity, fairness, and in an ethical manner. How can an individual person fulfill this role? Sergiovanni (2001) reminded us that leadership is a personal thing that is comprised of three important dimensions: one's *heart, head, and hand* [also cited as essential by Mary McLeod Bethune (Keough 2001)]. Working together these three dimensions will help the CKO (as well as the CFO and COO) fulfill the moral and ethical imperative, which is the successful education of all children.

Motivation

Rossow and Warner (2000) held that the role of the principal as motivator is one of the most significant roles that can be assumed by an effective instructional leader. The principal as CKO must know how to motivate not only teachers but also students. This skill for the instructional leader is tied to the concept of transformational leadership. Walker (1993) viewed transformational leadership as encompassing the following elements:

1. A collaborative, shared decision-making approach—these leaders believe that organizational goals can be better accomplished by shared commitment and collaboration.
2. An emphasis on teacher professionalism and teacher empowerment—these leaders believe that all teachers are capable of leadership and encourage them to be self-directed.
3. An understanding of change, including how to encourage change in others—these leaders are agents of change and are committed to educating students for this century.

When education is under attack from all fronts, dissension among the *ranks* will never lead to increased academic achievement for students. The CKO can do much to create a school climate of encouragement and support, moving quickly to seal cracks in a *wall* of declining morale that is becoming increasingly important to address in these times.

Decision-maker/ Planner

Sound decision-making and planning is key for the instructional leader. In this model of multi-leadership, decision-making is shared on many levels. Through this shared decision-making by all who have key roles (including the students) in the educational process, a sense of ownership is created and becomes a part of the culture of the school as an organization and community of practice.

Too often the educational blame game is played with parents blaming teachers, teachers blaming parents, as well as building level administrators blaming central office administration, teachers and parents. **In the game of blaming, the ultimate loser is the child.** The CKO can help all constituencies understand that making an educational decision that is sound will often require inviting people to the table that are not usually a part of the conversation yet are key stakeholders. This will require a great deal of strategic planning and of competent negotiation. This role can be monumental, but if an administrator understands this component of the multi-leadership model, and the administrator has a degree of efficacy with decision making and planning, then the benefits to the organizational structure of the school and the progress toward enhancing educational gains will be great.

Conclusion

Focusing on strengthening teaching and learning; programs for special needs students; assessment of teacher and student performance; professional development; data-driven decision-making; and accountability (Seyfarth 1999; IEL 2000), instructional leadership is an important aspect of the academic life of the school. Today's urban schools require new models for change, as society becomes even more complex in terms of leadership, technology, and governance. The CKO serves the school as the instructional leader. In the current educational context, this position is becoming even more necessary. The CKO should provide visionary leadership and foster effective communication. The CKO must serve as the leader for student learning (IEL 2000). Furthermore, this individual must also determine the most beneficial model that best fits the needs of their particular school. In addition, the CKO should be discerning and collaborative. Also, he or she should promote shared planning, problem solving, and evaluation. Collaboration is the key in bringing about this kind of change. At the heart of the matter we must remember: **students that are academically successful will ultimately have greater access and fuller participation in the democratic process. A decision to change to this multi-leadership model is not just for the sake of changing, but positions building level administrators to participate in better serving those who are at the core of education's genesis–the children.**

*Note: The author would like to thank Floyd D. Beachum (Doctoral Candidate—Program in Leadership Studies in the College of Education and Human Development at Bowling Green State University) for his contributions to this chapter.

Chapter 5:

Standards and the Multi-leadership Model

Introduction

Many school public school districts across the nation are experiencing a shortage in the ranks of educational administration, especially at the building level. Fenwick and Pierce (2001) noted that "as the student population of our public schools continues to grow and diversify—nearly 55% are African American or Hispanic—the need for school administrators through the year 2004 is expected to increase 10 to 20 percent" (p. 25). The projected shortages coupled with the growing demands of the position itself have in many areas surpassed the profession in efforts to meet those demands. Joe Schneider, Executive Secretary of the National Policy Board for Educational Administration (NPBEA), stated that "changing demographics, rising numbers of poor children, and heightened accountability for student achievement have made the administrators' job tougher" (NPBEA 2002). Concomitantly, principals already "in the trenches" are increasingly reporting that the job is simply not "doable" (IEL 2000). Administrative reform must move simultaneously alongside school reform and foster a (re)invention of the principalship as a vital component for the success of children in public education.

Skills and Standards

Discussions and delineations of a core knowledge base, skills, and national standards have become commonplace in our language and course of action regarding education in the 21st century. These conversations are not only taking place in K-12 policymaking settings, but also in leadership preparation programs as well. At this moment, the increased influence of standards' boards [state, national, professional] has shifted the rhetoric used to describe the preparation of school leaders (Drake and Roe 2003). A few organizations, in particular the National Policy Board for Educational Administration (NPBEA) and the Interstate School Leaders Licensure Consortium (ISLLC) along with the approval of the National Council for the Accreditation for Teacher Education (NCATE), have been leading the efforts. Both the NPBEA and ISLLC standards are discussed below.

NPBEA Standards

The National Policy Board for Educational Administration (NPBEA) offers seven standards (recently approved by NCATE in 2002) that will enable leadership preparation programs to ensure that their graduates have the necessary knowledge and skills to provide quality leadership for schools and school districts (NPBEA 2002). The newly revised standards, which mirror the ISLLC standards, are as follows:

> ➤ Candidates who complete the program are educational leaders who have the knowledge and ability to promote the success of all students by facilitating the development, articulation, implementation, and stewardship of a school or district vision of learning supported by the school community.
> ➤ Candidates who complete the program are educational leaders who have the knowledge and ability to promote the success of all students by promoting a positive school culture, providing an effective instructional program, applying best practice to student learning, and designing comprehensive professional growth plans for staff.
> ➤ Candidates who complete the program are educational leaders who have the knowledge and ability to promote the success of all students by managing the organization, operations, and resources in a way that promotes a safe, efficient, and effective learning environment.

➤ Candidates who complete the program are educational leaders who have the knowledge and ability to promote the success of all students by collaborating with families and other community members, responding to diverse community interests and needs, and mobilizing community resources.

➤ Candidates who complete the program are educational leaders who have the knowledge and ability to promote the success of all students by acting with integrity, fairly, and in an ethical manner.

➤ Candidates who complete the program are educational leaders who have the knowledge and ability to promote the success of all students by understanding, responding to, and influencing the larger political, social, economic, legal, and cultural context.

➤ Internship. The internship provides significant opportunities for candidates to synthesize and apply the knowledge and practice and develop the skills identified in Standards 1-6 through substantial, sustained, standards-based work in real settings, planned and guided cooperatively by the institution and school district personnel for graduate credit.

ISLLC Standards

The list of standards for school leaders provided by the Interstate School Leaders Licensure Consortium (ISLLC) was adopted by the Council of Chief State School Officers (CCSSO) in 1996.

The standards present a common core of knowledge, dispositions, and performances that will help link leadership more forcefully to productive schools and enhanced educational outcomes...they represent another part of a concerted effort to enhance the skills of school leaders and to couple leadership with effective educational processes and valued outcomes. (CCSSO 1996, 3)

These standards are as follows:

A school administrator is an educational leader who promotes the success of all students by:

1. facilitating the development, articulation, implementation, and stewardship of a vision of learning that shared and supported by the school community.
2. advocating, nurturing, and sustaining a school culture and instructional program conducive to student learning and staff professional growth.

3 . ensuring management of the organization, operations, and resources for a safe, efficient, and effective learning environment.
4 . collaborating with families and community members, responding to diverse community interests and needs, and mobilizing community resources.
5. acting with integrity, fairness, and in an ethical manner.
6 . understanding, responding to, and influencing the larger political, social, economic, legal, and cultural context.

These standards promote professionalism, accountability, and hold educational leaders' collective *feet to the fire*. These standards provide a means to benchmark effective leadership and to provide a *blueprint* for individual and collective professional growth and development. Moving from an overview of the standards to a more finite look at the Alston Model of Multi-leadership (see Fig. 1.1) provides an integrated approach for a coherent critique of these ideals.

Model of Multi-leadership and the ISLLC standards

The model for multi-leadership fundamentally evokes a theoretical as well as practical view of the principalship. It is related to the common sensibility needed to successfully support the many roles of a building principal in a given workday. The eclectic responsibilities that contemporary, albeit 21st century principals, are becoming increasingly accountable for can best be supported by a three- or four-prong approach with specificity to leadership.

The ISLLC standards are grounded in the philosophy and application of effective schools. A large body of research supports that effective school reform initiatives lead to increases in academic success for all children. The implications for effective school reform can not, as it has historically, stop with curriculum and instruction. The multifaceted leadership model brings to the standards (Fig. 5.1) the *specificity* needed not only for implementation of effective school reform but also the guiding principles for implementation of the standards, resulting in improved leadership outcomes, coupled with judicious accountablity.

For instance, you may have blueprints (guiding principles) for a home, but if the city building codes for a specific land catchment area, specific sewage codes, and specific electrical codes (standards) are not met, the building will be halted until the builder meets with each responsible party. This can work with schools as well. Much like city hall separates the responsibility for each building code in individual departments and offices, to separate the daily school operations from the fiscal responsibilities or fiscal responsibilities from the development of pedagogical knowledge, each person is given the opportunity to bring expertise to the job at hand with fewer distractions and increased efficiency. Efficiency in management coupled with school leadership leads to an effective matriculation of the overall operation of a given school.

Figure 5.1

ISSLC Standard	Major Player*		
	CKO	COO	CFO
1. Facilitating the development, articulation, implementation, and stewardship of a vision of learning that shared and supported by the school community.	√	√	√
2. Advocating, nurturing, and sustaining a school culture and instructional program conducive to student learning and staff professional growth.	√		
3. Ensuring management of the organization, operations, and resources for a safe, efficient, and effective learning environment.		√	
4. Collaborating with families and community members, responding to diverse community interests and needs, and mobilizing community resources			√
5. Acting with integrity, fairness, and in an ethical manner.	√	√	√
6. Understanding, responding to, and influencing the larger political, social, economic, legal, and cultural context.		√	

*Note: While all members of the leadership team would encounter opportunities to demonstrate competency of each standard at any given time, the benefits of uninterrupted priority by one member of the multi-leadership team given to specific areas of leadership over time will support a space for greater focus and efficiency.

The ISLLC standards at the very core deal with the many facets of effective leadership. The principles are written broadly enough to embrace the various personal leadership styles of individuals and allow for the adaptation to the sociopolitical context of each school community. While standards must be written vaguely for the widest application, this often leads to ineffective implementation, and ultimately becomes an accountability issue. For example, as stated in earlier chapters, the demographics of this country support that the diversity of the nation is showing up in the classrooms of the 21st century. Those in educational administration are now faced with the challenges in the form of legislative bills and acts that are a result of increased poverty, school violence, immigration and migration of refugees, and federal responses to low performance on standardized tests. We know that legislation is not sufficient. We need only to bear in mind our shared historical memory of times past when the playing field was not level for all who were American to participate fully in the educational enterprise. The passing of legislation did not ensure that the *spirit* of the law showed up in the classrooms of America. The story of Ruby Bridges, the six-year-old little girl, captured in a Norman Rockwell painting, as the first black child to evoke her right to attend an all white school, walked with armed National Guardsmen into her first grade classroom. This created an indelible mark in our minds that taught us that more than legislation is needed if we are going to get serious results in the arena of equity and social justice in schools.

Conclusion

So, what can we do? Achilles and Price (2001) argued the following:

> A valid and powerful set of standards for EDAD [Educational Administration] must include those elements embodied in a strong well-defined KB [Knowledge Base] which provides the structure and expertise for the profession. We also argue—and agree with ISLLC—that knowing and being able to use effective leadership skills such as facilitating, advocating, collaborating, maintaining high moral and ethical behavior, etc., are key elements in being able to put in place programs and practices that work for children. Standards that ignore one or the other will do little to advance EDAD and most importantly, will not result in school improvement. (p. 12)

Additionally, while the standards do not deal directly with diversity, the Alston Model of Multi-leadership can help to fill that gap in several ways. A team approach to leadership would afford school districts the opportunity to increase the diversity in leadership positions. When only one principal or even two (if there is an assistant principal) are in place, they are more often than not male and white. A commitment to diversity in the filling of the multi-leadership model would increase the chances that the leadership team will reflect the demographics of the school district and nation.

Based on these gaps, while these standards are nice to have, in many ways they continue to promote the status quo. This can be addressed in how leadership preparation programs train and provide professional growth for leaders.

Epilogue

Multi-leadership in Action:
As the Day Turns

It's 1:00 p.m. and my grandmother and I are outside talking over the backyard fence to a neighbor, Just like clockwork the emergency broadcast system sounds the test alarm. My grandmother and her friend bid each other a quick good bye and retreat to their television sets as they have for the last 20 years to spend thirty minutes, suspending belief, watching a daily soap opera, *As the World Turns*. Every episode of the daytime drama ends with cliffhangers that lead into new problems, new solutions, and new discoveries.

Each day in today's educational arena an " administrative drama" unfolds in the elementary, middle, and high schools that requires suspending belief, dealing with yesterday's cliffhanger(s) in the face of new problems, new solutions, and often ending with a continuing cliffhanger to usher in a new day. The multi-leadership model offers a division of labor that would elevate the overwhelmed individual administrator in lieu of a development of expertise in the sharing of the responsibilities that often mirror organizations in the corporate world. This is not to suggest, as some have that a business model of leadership and operations is what is needed in schools today. Nevertheless, there are some aspects of business models that are not only applicable but also needed for school leadership. Schools are not corporations and students are not employees or clients. Schools are places where contexts of learning are created and supported, places where responding to the individual needs of young people whose lives often hang in the balance, and places where academic achievement can accrue academic capital that in the new millennium is a criteria for life success.

The short descriptions below offer an opportunity to examine the real life examples of everyday school administrator life, with a view to the Alston Model of Multi-leadership. Where could each of these administrators use a COO to take care of the general and specific operations of the building? Or act as the CKO and offer instructional leadership to a teacher, student or academic enrichment activity advisor? Or a CFO to deal with a mountain of paper work related to the financial responsibilities? On each level, the model is apropos and open to full or partial application.

Elementary Principal:

Arrive at 6:40. Get organized. Call to the system to see which teachers are absent (no secretary since January). Put the school mail that arrives at 7:00 in staff mailboxes. Respond to email requests for information from central administration. Morning meeting with staff at 8:15 – 8:30. Monitor students coming into the building 9:00 - 3:00. Deal with discipline issues (Two 3rd graders fighting over an incident with the jump rope from yesterday), contact each 4th grade parent of students who did not pass the reading proficiency test. Send letters home to each student and give each student summer school information. Deal with a fight that occurred yesterday after school, and do an investigation. Take care of any money issues regarding popcorn sales, documenting receipts for the school treasurer and try to deal with the copier company who wants to charge a fee that had no authorization. Meet with the school treasurer at 1:15 and exchange paperwork and make budget plans for next year. Still having to answer numerous telephone calls, go through the US mail, which arrives at 2:00. Numerous teachers want "just a minute" of your time, which equals about an hour. (A minute usually means 5-10 minutes.) Again, monitor halls and cafeteria/playground during lunchtime (teachers having some issues with lunch duty). At 4:00 start the new teacher interview process for next year and finally wrap up interviews at 8:20 p.m. Walk back up to the office and try to clear off my desk and do "paperwork" for about another 1.5 hours. Go home 10:00 p.m.

Middle School Principal:

5:00 AM	Time to hit the floor and get ready for the workday
6:30 AM	Depart for school
7:40 AM	Arrive at school
	Review calendar for scheduled parent/teacher conferences, meetings, etc.
	Coffee
	Check in with Cafeteria Manager (note left for me about oven door being out of balance and serviceman had not come to fix the problem)
8:00 AM	Head Custodian stops by and reviews schedule for summer cleaning

Talk with students at the entrance about arriving at
school too early
Phone call from citizen in the neighborhood (students
at bus stop picking flowers from her yard. She did
not have names but described one of the boy wearing
a red baseball shirt. This is at the corner of Central
and Green Road. She wanted me to make sure that
this does not happen again.)

8:30 AM Working the hallways (talking with teacher(s) about
testing, concern about data being accurate. Would
like to have test re-scored.)

8:55AM Called to the office (one student had a problem on the
bus, driver and student waiting to see me. Requested
driver to write a bus complaint on student)

9:10 AM Rounds in the classrooms (Started today with four
Occupational Handicap classrooms, two 7^h grade
classrooms)
Called to office (Classified Personnel office returning
my call from yesterday).

9:45 AM Back to making classrooms rounds. (Starting with
three 8th grade classrooms, interviewed by 8th grade
students for their journal writing (interview was not
planned for; provided written feedback to this
teacher).
Continued with classrooms rounds (walkthroughs)

10:00 AM. Scheduled parent conference
Talked with Literacy Facilitator about one student

10:20 AM. Brief conversation with secretary about Requisitions.

10:20 AM EMERGENCY—called to office-my child fell at
school, arm may be broken. Left for day. "Teacher-
on-duty" left in charge. (No AP's) *Note-"Teacher-
on-duty" can not do any formal "principal" work;
just keep the building running. If anything major
(suspensions, fights, etc.) or even some minor issues
(accepting packages), must call another principal or
area supervisor.*

High School Principal:
3:45 AM Alarm sounds
5:30 AM Arrive to the office, turn on computer and perform
initial check of email and Lotus Notes calendar, and

	private meditation.
6:45 AM	Teachers begin to arrive and "drop in" to talk
6:55 AM	Students begin to arrive
7:05 AM	Morning duty until the start of school
7:30 AM	Block 1: Work block…work on correspondence and other district requested information.
9:00 AM	Class Break: Hallway Duty
9:15 AM	Block 2: Available for teachers, students, and parents
10:40 AM	Block 3: Cafeteria duty for lunch blocks; Toilet busted in the boys locker room; basketball game scheduled this afternoon
1:00 PM	Block 4: Available for teachers, students, and parents Irate parents show up at office demanding to see me about their daughters and sons not being chosen for the cheerleading squad. Major issues!
2:30 PM	Students depart and After-school Academy, Extra Help and Evening classes begin. It is the responsibility of the administrative team to clear the hallways and monitor students' comings and goings. Still dealing with the cheerleading situation. Have to call the superintendent's office
3:00 PM	Work in office. Return phone calls, field questions from teachers, address other staff-related issues.
5:00 PM	From 5pm on, generally three nights per week there are supervision* duties of athletic, extra-curricular, and co-curricular programs.
9:00 PM	Home from all activities. From 9-10 check email and review mail and signature folder
10:00pm	Go to bed

*Note: On non-supervision days, I am able to go home by 4pm. During the course of the school year, there are approximately 10-15 weekend activities that require administrative supervision.

References

Achilles, C.M. and W.J. Price. 2001. What is missing in the current debate about education administration (EDAD) standards! *The AASA Professor*, 24: 8-14.

Alston, J.A. 1999. Missing from action: The lack of black female school superintendents. *Urban Education*, 35: 525-531.

Alston, J.A. and S.N. Jones. 2001. Carrying the torch of the Jeanes supervisors: 21st century African American female superintendents and servant leadership. *The promise and perils of today's school superintendent*, edited by B.S. Cooper and L.D. Fusarelli, 65-75. Lanham, MD: Scarecrow Press.

Andrews, R. L. and R. Soder. 1987. Principal leadership and student achievement. *Educational Leadership*, 44: 9-11.

Armstrong, D.G., K.T. Henson, and T.V. Savage. 2001. *Teaching today*. Upper Saddle River, NJ: Merrill Prentice Hall.

Ash, R. C. and J.M. Persall. 2000. The principal as chief learning officer: Developing teachers. *NASSP Bulletin*, 84: 15-22.

Ayers, W. 1994. Can city schools be saved? *Educational Leadership*, 51: 60-63.

Barth, R.S. 1988. Principals, teachers, and school leadership. *Phi Delta Kappan*, 69: 639-641.

Beck, L. and J. Murphy. 1993. *Understanding the principalship*. New York: Teachers College Press.

Bennis, W. and B. Nanus. 1985. *Leaders: The strategies for taking charge*. New York: Harper and Row.

Blackmore, J. 1989. Changes from within: Feminist educators and administrative leadership. *Peabody Journal of Education*, 66: 19-40.

Boyd, B. 1996. The principal as teacher: A model for instructional leadership. *NASSP Bulletin* 80: 65.

Bredeson, P. 1989. An analysis of the metaphorical perspectives of school principals. *School leadership: A contemporary reader*, edited by J. Burdin, 297-317. Newbury Park, CA: Sage.

Buffie, E.G. 1989. *The principal and leadership*. Bloomington, IN: Phi Delta Kappa Educational Foundation.

Burrup, P.E., V. Brimley, Jr., and R.R. Garfield. 1999. *Financing education in a climate of change*. Boston, MA: Allyn and Bacon.

Chapman, J. 1993. Leadership, management and the effectiveness of schooling: A response to Mr. Gradgrind. *Journal of Educational Administration*, 31: 4-18.

Christ, S.E. 1994. *The meaning of leadership to women in higher education*. Unpublished doctoral dissertation. The Pennsylvania State University.

Cook, M.L. 1980. The development of leaders from the ranks of labor. *Business leadership*, edited by H.E. Metcalf, New York: Isaac Pitman and Sons.

Council of Chief State Officers. 1996. *Interstate school leaders licensure consortium: Standards for school leaders.* Washington, DC: Council of Chief State School Officers.

Cox, T., Jr. 1993. *Cultural diversity in organizations: Theory, research and practice.* San Francisco: Berrett-Koehler.

Daresh, J.C. 2002. *What it means to be a principal: Your guide to leadership.* Thousand Oaks, CA: Corwin Press, Inc.

Deal, T. and K. Peterson. 1991. *The principal's role in shaping school culture.* Washington, DC: U.S. Department of Education, Office of Educational Research and Improvement.

Digest of education statistics. 2002. *Digest of education statistics.* Washington, DC: National Center for Education Statistics

Dinham, S., T. Cairney, D. Craigie, and S. Wilson. 1995. School climate and leadership: Research into three secondary schools. *Journal of Educational Administration,* 33: 36-58.

Donaldson Jr., G.A. 2001. *Cultivating leadership in schools: Connecting people, purpose, and practice.* New York: Teachers College Press.

Drake, T.L. and W.H. Roe. (1999). *The principalship.* (5th edition). Columbus, OH: Merrill Prentice Hall.

_____. (2003). *The principalship.* (6th edition). Columbus, OH: Merrill Prentice Hall.

Drath, W.H. 1998. Approaching the future of leadership development. *The center for creative leadership handbook of leadership development,* edited by In C.D. McCauley, R.S. Moxley, and E.Van Velsor. San Francisco, CA: Jossey-Bass Publishers.

Drath W.H. and C.J. Palus. 1994. *Making common sense: Leadership as meaning-making in a community of practice.* Greensboro, NC: Center for Creative Leadership.

Edmonds, R. 1979. Effective schools for the urban poor. *Educational Leadership,* 37: 15-24.

Fenwick, L.T. and M.C. Pierce. 2001. The principal shortage: Crisis or opportunity? *Principal,* 80: 24-32.

Firestone, W.A. 1996. Images of teaching and proposals for reform: A comparison of ideas from cognitive and organizational research. *Educational Administration Quarterly,* 32: 209-235.

Fredericks, J. 1992. Ongoing principal development: The route to restructuring urban schools. *Education and Urban Society,* 25: 57-70.

Frohreich, L.E. 1983. *The school budgeting cycle* (3rd Edition). Winneconne, WI: Wisconsin Association of School Boards.

Fullan, M. 1998, April. Breaking the bonds of dependency. *Educational Leadership,* 55: 6-10.

Gainey, D. 1993. *Education for the new century: Views from the principal's office.* Reston, VA: NASSP.

Hallinger, P. and J.F. Murphy. 1987. Assessing and developing principal instructional leadership. *Educational Leadership,* 8: 54-61.

Hart, L.B. 1980. *Moving up! Women and leadership.* New York: Amacom.

Heenan, D. A. and W. Bennis. 1999. *Co-Leaders*. New York: John Wiley and
    Sons, Inc.
Hess, F. M. 1999. *Spinning wheels: The politics of urban school reform.*
    Washington, D.C.: Brookings Institution Press.
Hoerr, T. R. 1996. Collegiality: A new way to define instructional leadership.
    Phi Delta Kappan, 77: 380.
Institute for Educational Leadership (IEL). 2000. *Leadership for student
    learning: Reinventing the principalship.* Washington, DC: Institute of
    Educational Leadership, Inc.
Kennedy, C. 2001. Splitting the principalship. *Principal,* 80:60.
Keough, L. 2001. "Mary McLeod Bethune." 2 June 2001,
    <http://www.africana.com?Articles/tt_904.htm> (10 July 2002).
Kimbrough, R.B. and C.W. Burkett. 1990. The principalship: *Concepts and
    practices.* Englewood Cliffs, NJ: Prentice Hall.
Kouzes, J. M. and B.Z. Posner. 1995. *The leadership challenge.* San Francisco:
    Jossey-Bass.
Lave, J. and E. Wenger. 1991. *Situated learning: Legitimate peripheral
    participation.* Cambridge, MA: Harvard University Press.
Lightfoot, S.L. 1983. *The good high school: Portraits of character and
    culture.* New York: Basic Books.
Lipham, J. M., R.E. Rankin, and J.A. Hoeh, Jr. 1985. *The principalship:
    Concepts, competencies and cases.* New York: Longman Publishers.
Logophilia Limited, "Chief Knowledge Officer," 12 June 1998,
    <http://www.logophilia.com/WordSpy/chiefknowledgeofficer.asp.>
    (20 January 2002).
Lomotey, K. 1989. *African-American principals: School leadership and
    success.* New York: Greenwood Press.
Marion, R. 2002. *Leadership in education: Organizational theory for the
    practitioner.* UpperSaddle River, NJ: Merrill Prentice Hall.
Meyers, K. and G. Pawlas. 1989. *The principal and discipline.* Bloomington,
    IN: Phi Delta Kappa Educational Foundation.
Murphy, J. 2001, Winter. The changing face of schools and principals. *Ohio
    CES Newsletter,* 1-3.
Neilson, R.E. "Role of the CKO," May 2001,
    <http://www.ndu.edu/irmc/km-cio-role/km-cio-role.htm> (20 June
    2002.
NPBEA. 2002. "Revised standards for the review of university-based programs
    in educational administration receive approval." 20 February 2002,
    <http://www.npbea.org/ELCC/index.html> (5 July 2002).
O'Reilly, C.A. and J.A. Chatman. 1996. Culture as social control:
    Corporations, cults, and commitment. *Research in Organizational
    Behavior,* edited by B.M. Shaw and L.L. Cummings, 18. Greenwich,
    CT: JAI Press.
Oswald, L. 1995. *Priority on learning: Efficient use of resources.* Eugene,
    OR: ERIC Clearinghouse on Educational management. (ERIC
    Document Reproduction Service No. ED 384 951).

Owens, R.G. 1995. Leadership. *Organizational behavior in education*, edited by R. Short, 115-143. Needham Heights, MA: Simon and Shuster.

Patterson, J. 1993. *Principal leadership and student achievement.* Alexandria, VA: Association for Supervision and Curriculum Development.

Peterson, K.D. 1987. An organizational perspective on career movement. *Administrator's Notebook*, 32: 1-4.

Phi Delta Kappa Commission on Discipline 1982. *Handbook for developing schools with good discipline.* Bloomington, IN: Phi Delta Kappa.

Pierce, M. 2000, September/October. Portrait of the super principal. *Harvard Education Letter Research Online.*

Razik, T.A. and A.D. Swanson. 2001. *Fundamental concepts of educational leadership* (2nd edition). Columbus, OH: Merrill Prentice-Hall.

Riggins, C.G. 2001. The urban principal: Lone Ranger no more. *Principal*, 80: 27.

Rossow, L.E. and L.S. Warner. 2000. *The principalship: Dimensions in instructional leadership* (2nd edition). Durham, NC: Carolina Academic Press.

Sanders, E.T.W. 1999. *Urban school leadership: Issues and Strategies.* Larchmont, NY: Eye on Education.

Sarason, S.B. 1982. *The culture of the school and the problem of change.* Boston, MA: Allyn and Bacon.

Schein, E.H. 1992. *Organizational culture and leadership* (2nd edition.). San Francisco, CA: Jossey-Bass.

Schlechty, P.C. 1997. *Inventing better schools: An action plan for educational reform.* San Francisco, CA: Jossey-Bass.

Sergiovanni, T.J. 1992. *Moral leadership: Getting to the heart of school improvement.* San Francisco, CA: Jossey-Bass.

_____. 1996. *Leadership for the schoolhouse.* San Francisco, CA: Jossey-Bass.

_____. 2001. *The principalship: A reflective practice perspective.* Needham Heights, MA: Allyn and Bacon.

Sergiovanni, T.J., M. Burlingame, F.S. Coombs, and P.W. Thurston. 1999. *Educational governance and administration.* Needham Heights, MA: Allyn and Bacon.

Seyfarth, J.T. 1999. *The principal: New directions for new challenges.* Upper Saddle River, NJ: Merrill Prentice-Hall.

Short, P.M. and J.T. Greer. 2002. *Leadership in empowered schools: Themes from innovative efforts.* Upper Saddle River, NJ: Prentice Hall.

Short, P. M. and W.A. Spencer. 1990. Principal instructional leadership. *Journal of Research and Development in Education*, 23:177-121.

Sizer, T.R. 1985. *Horace's compromise: The dilemma of the American high school.* Boston, MA: Houghton Mifflin.

Stewart, R. 1982. The relevance of some studies of managerial work and behavior to leadership research. *Leadership beyond establishment views*, edited by J.G. Hunt, U. Sekaran, and C.A. Schriesheim Carbondale, IL: Southern Illinois University.

Smith, D.M. and E.A. Holdaway. 1995. Constraints on the effectiveness of schools and their principals. *International Journal of Educational Management,* 9: 6-7.

Tagiuri, R. 1968. The concept of organizational climate. *Organizational climate: Exploration of a concept,* edited by R. Tagiuri and G.H. Litwin . Boston, MA: Harvard University, Division of Research, Graduate School of Business Management.

Tead, O. 1930. The leader as coordinator. *Business leadership,* edited by H.C. Metcalf. New York: Isaac Pitman and Sons.

Thurston, P., R. Clift, R. and M. Schacht. 1993. Preparing leaders for change-oriented schools. *Phi Delta Kappan,* 75: 259-265.

Urban School Services. "Definition of Urban" (no date). <http://www.acsi.org/services/urban/definition.cfm> 14 January 2002.

Vandenberghe, R. 1995. Creative management of a school: A matter of vision and daily interventions. *Journal of Educational Administration,* 33: 31-51.

Walker, D. 1993. Developing transformational leaders. *Thrust for Educational Leadership,* 22: 34-35.

Walter, J.K. and G.D. Marconnit. 1989. *The principal and fiscal management.* Bloomington, IN: Phi Delta Kappa Educational Foundation.

Weiner, L. 1999. *Urban teaching: The essentials.* New York: Teachers College Press.

Whitaker, B. 1997. Instructional leadership and principal visibility. *The Clearing House* 70: 155-156.

White, R. P., P. Hodgson, and S. Cramer. 1996. *The future of leadership: Riding the corporate rapids into the 21st century.* Washington, DC: Pitman Publishing.

Wohlstetter, P. and S.A. Mohrman. 1994, December. School-based management: Promise and process. *CPRE Finance Briefs.*

Woolf, H.B. (Ed.). 1974. *The Merriam-Webster dictionary.* New York: Pocket Books.

Yukl, G.A. 1991. *Leadership in organizations.* Englewood Cliffs, NJ: Prentice-Hall, Inc.

Zhang, Y. 1994. Leadership attributes in a cultural setting in Singapore. *International Journal of Educational Management,* 8: 16-18.

Index

About the Author

A native of Charleston, SC, Judy A. Alston, serves as the Chair of the Program in Educational Administration and Supervision, as well as an Assistant Professor in that program and in the Doctoral Program in Leadership Studies at Bowling Green State University. In 1987 she completed her Bachelors degree in English at Winthrop College (now University) in Rock Hill, SC; in 1990 and 1992, two Masters degrees at the University of South Carolina (Columbia) and her Ph.D. in 1996 at The Pennsylvania State University (University Park). Prior to teaching in the academy, she was a high school English teacher in the public school system in Berkeley County and Lexington School District #2, both in South Carolina.

Dr. Alston teaches courses in School Supervision and Staff Development, Diversity and Leadership, and Leadership and Adult Development. Her research interests include black female school superintendents, issues of diversity and leadership, and women and leadership.